EVERY TEENAGER SHOULD KNOW

31 verses

ExodusLeviticusNumbersDeutero... ...aJudgesRuth1Samuel2Samuel1Kings2Kings ...s2Chronicle
stherJobPsalmsProverbsEcclesi... ...gofSolomonIsaiahJeremiahLamentationsEzekielDa... ...JoelAmo
MicahNahumHabakkukZephani... ...nZechariahMalachiMatthewMarkLukeJohnActsRoman... ...nians2Cc
sEphesiansPhilippiansColossi... ...ssalonians2Thessalonians1Timothy2TimothyTitusPhilem... ...wsJame
r1John2John3JohnJudeRevel... ...nesisExodusLeviticusNumbersDeuteronomyJoshuaJudges... ...amuel2
Kings1Chronicles2Chronicles... ...her...John...Prov...D...s...ngof...d... ...Jerem
sEzekielDanielHoseaJoel... ...o...hMa...nHabakk... ...aiZe...riahM... ...tthew
nActsRomans1Corinthians2C... ...tia...Eph...ainsPhilipp...ans... ...essalonians2... ...onian

THE BIBLE

By
Andy Blanks &
Melanie Dill

© 2008 SL Resources, Inc.

Published by SL Resources, Inc.
Student Life
2183 Parkway Lake Drive
Hoover, AL 35244

www.studentlife.com

ISBN-10: 1-935040-02-2
ISBN-13: 1-935040-02-6

31 Verses Every Teenager Should Know™

TABLE
of
CONTENTS

As recent as April 2008, a national poll conducted by Reuters found that the Bible is still the most popular book among adults in the United States.

What does that even mean?

Bands and singers are popular. Could you sing the words to every song on Hannah Montana's *Non-Stop Dance Party*? I thought you could. Sports teams are popular. Fashion trends are popular. Celebrities are popular. Without thinking, name five celebrities the world knows on a first-name basis. (Did you say Paris, Britney, Angelina, Brad, and Lindsay?)

Is the Bible popular like these things are popular? I'm willing to go out on a limb and say that it's not. And you know what? Maybe it shouldn't be. Our relationship with the Bible should be different from our relationship with other books and other forms of entertainment. Why? Because the Bible isn't like other books.

The Bible is literally the collected words of God. It is His story. It is His chosen way to communicate His love and grace and justice and compassion and judgment and forgiveness to His chosen people.

The question, then, is do you know your Bible? If you know your Bible pretty well, this little book will help you know it more. If you would like to know your Bible better, this book is a great place to start. By studying through the next 31 verses, you will learn how the Bible *describes* God's Word, how we are to *respond* to God's Word, how we are to *believe* in God's Word, and how we are to *live* God's Word. That's a lot to accomplish, right? This book is proof that big things *do* come in small packages . . .

My prayer is that the words of this book will lead you to spend more time with the words of *the* Book.

God Bless,
Andy Blanks

Now that you own this incredible little book, you may be wondering, "What do I do with it?"

Glad you asked . . . The great thing about this book is that you can use it just about any way you want.

It's not a system. It's a resource that can be used in ways that are as unique and varied as you are.

A few suggestions . . .

The "One Month" Plan
On this plan, you'll read one devotional each day for a month. This is a great way to immerse yourself in the Bible for a month-long period. (OK, we realize that every month doesn't have 31 days. But 30 is close enough to 31, right?) The idea is to cover a lot of information in a short amount of time.

The "Scripture Memory" Plan
The idea behind this plan is to memorize the verse for each day's devotional; you don't move on to the next devotional until you have memorized the one you're on. If you're like most people, this might take you more than one day per devotional. So, this plan takes a slower approach.

The "I'm No Charles Dickens" Plan
Don't like to write or journal? This plan is for you . . . Listen, not everyone expresses themselves the same. If you don't like to express yourself through writing, that's OK. Simply read the devotional for each verse, then read the questions. Think about them. Pray through them. But don't feel like you have to journal if you don't want to.

The "Strength In Numbers" Plan
God designed humans for interaction. We are social animals. How cool would it be if you could go through "31:The Bible" with your friends? Get a group of friends together. Consider agreeing to read five verses each week, then meeting to talk about it.

Pretty simple, right? Choose a plan. Or make up your own. But get started already. What are you waiting on?

> "For the word of God is living and active. Sharper than any double-edged sword, it penetrates even to dividing soul and spirit, joints and marrow; it judges the thoughts and attitudes of the heart."
> **Hebrews 4:12**

If you let down your guard and are honest for a moment you might agree to the following statement: Studying the Bible can be hard. If you agree, you're not alone. Every Christian has struggled at times with digging into God's Word. Sometimes it can feel like the equivalent of doing homework. But the comparison to homework ends here. You see, while the Bible can seem challenging at times, one important difference sets it apart from any textbook.

Read Hebrews 4:12. This verse holds the key to what makes the Bible different from any other book ever written. The Bible is not merely words. It is alive—literally. The picture of the Word as a sharp sword is powerful! A sword is a weapon, a tool, a divisive instrument. It cuts to the heart of every individual, exposing the good and the bad.

Have you ever read the Bible and felt convicted of things you needed to change about your life? If so, then you know the Bible is capable of judging your thoughts and attitudes. Not only that, it is capable of encouraging you and leading you to change your heart.

Knowing God's Word is essential to your relationship with Him. There really is no way around it. If you claim to love the Lord, believe in His death and resurrection, and have accepted Christ as your Savior, you cannot afford to miss out on the living, active story contained in His Word.

God is calling you to know Him. His Word is the most complete way of doing this. Will you accept the call?

REFLECT

1. Why do you sometimes find it hard to study the Bible? What can you do to help limit things that make studying Scripture difficult?

2. How is God's Word active in your life?

3. Describe a time when the Word has helped you judge your thoughts and attitudes.

4. Pray that God would open your heart to what He has to say to you. Write a short prayer asking Him to teach you today through His active Word.

"Do not add to what I command you and do not subtract from it, but keep the commands of the LORD your God that I give you."
Deuteronomy 4:2

So you want to impress your date, and you decide to cook your mom's famous crispy pork cutlets with capers, lemon, arugula, and chopped eggs. "It's a sure fire hit," you say to yourself. But as you look over the ingredients, you realize the recipe does not call for your favorite food: french fries. So, you toss in a handful of fries to spice things up. Also, you had a bad experience with pork once. So, you decide to take out the pork.

Read Deuteronomy 4:1–2. After 40 years of wandering in the wilderness as punishment for doubting Him, God finally allowed the Israelites to enter into the land He promised them. Before they went in, however, Moses read the Israelites all of the laws God had given them. These laws governed the way the Israelites worshiped and related to God. Moses clearly instructed the people not to add or take away from the Lord's words.

Adding french fries to a gourmet recipe ruins it. So does attempting to add something to God's Word. How do people add to God's Word? By trying to make personal preferences or church traditions as important as the Bible. As a guide for living the Christian life, the Bible is sufficient. It does not need any help in teaching us how to live godly lives.

Taking away from the Bible is just as bad. How does this happen? By choosing to obey or teach some parts of Scripture but not others. All of God's Word is vitally important. Do not make the mistake of thinking that the Bible needs anything from us. Exactly as it is, the Word has the power to change lives, history, and culture. Its truth is always relevant.

REFLECT

1. Why is it valuable to know God's Word well enough to know if someone is teaching something that adds or takes away from it?

2. Look back at the second part of the verse. What were the Israelites encouraged to do with the commands of God?

3. Consider your relationship with God's Word. Do you faithfully obey His teachings? What changes do you need to make today to be more obedient to His teachings?

4. Write a prayer to God asking for Him to help you to know when you are not obeying His Word and to give you the strength to stand up to temptation.

"The law of the LORD is perfect, reviving the soul. The statutes of the LORD are trustworthy, making wise the simple."
Psalm 19:7

Think for a moment about the different rules you might encounter in your life. No text messaging in class. No driving on the Interstate until you turn 17. No talking on the phone after 10 p.m. No spending the night at a friend's house when his or her parents are out of town. How do these rules make you feel? While they are mostly made to protect you, they still bum you out, right? Rules can do that. Most of them seem made to keep you from having fun or expressing yourself.

Read Psalm 19. David, the writer of this particular psalm, declares how great the Lord is by praising His creation (vv. 1–6). He then speaks highly of the Scriptures (vv. 7–8, 11), and praises the judgment of the Lord (vv. 9–11). David reminds us that even God's judgments of us are "more precious than gold . . . sweeter than honey (v. 10)." These are powerful words of affirmation spoken to a God who is bigger and greater than we can ever truly fathom.

Pay close attention to what David says in verse 7. Look how he describes God's Law. David says the laws, or rules, of God revive his soul. Wow! When could you last say that about a rule? But that's the deal with God. His lordship over us revives us. In the world, being a servant to a master leads to depression. But being a servant to the Master brings life.

Perfect. Reviving. Trustworthy. Wise. What hopeful words! There are not many people or things in this world that we can say encompass all of these qualities. God's Word is greater than anything made by human hands, more perfect than anything we know.

1. Write about a time you may have doubted God and did not obey His prompting.

2. Why did you doubt Him? Did it have anything to do with pride or embarrassment?

3. Has the Word of God ever "revived your soul"? Describe a situation when you have read the Word and felt encouraged.

4. Psalm 19:14 is a great prayer from David. Make it your prayer today as you trust God's Word and obey Him. Rewrite Psalm 19:14 in your own words as a prayer to God.

"Your word is a lamp to my feet and a light for my path."
Psalm 119:105

Were you afraid of the dark as a kid? That is OK . . . you weren't alone. A lot of people feared the dark. And let's be honest . . . even now that you're older, hanging out in the dark is not cool at all. Think of the last time you were in a really dark place, as in the kind of darkness where you couldn't see your hand in front of your face; the kind that makes you stand still, as if you're frozen; the kind that makes you imagine sounds and noises that aren't really there. There's nothing fun about that kind of darkness.

Read Psalm 119:105–112. This section of Psalm 119 seems to come from the voice of someone going through a struggle, or a trying time. Look closely: In verse 107 the author says, "I have suffered much"; in verse 109 he says "I constantly take my life in my hands"; in verse 110 he talks about wicked people setting a trap for him. This guy seems to really have some problems! But in verse 105 the author confesses that God's Word sees him through. God's Word was the secret to his survival. Like a lamp, it brings light to a path darkened by fear and uncertainty.

Don't you find it comforting having the Word as "a lamp" to guide you? Think about it: if you are in a really dark place, don't you want something to light a path for you? This analogy of God's Word as a light helps us realize that Scripture is a guide and a director, something to give us comfort.

When you study God's Word and apply it to your life, have confidence in its ability to light your path in what can sometimes seem a dark, fearful world.

1. Make a list of things that can darken the paths of your life.

2. Journal about a time when God's Word brought you guidance, peace, happiness, or comfort during a trying time.

3. What kind of confidence in Scripture does the author's hope in the midst of trying times give you?

4. Write a prayer to the Lord today thanking Him for giving His Word to lift you up when you face the darkness. Ask Him to help you hide His Word in your heart so that you will have it with you when you most need it.

"For these commands are a lamp, this teaching is a light, and the corrections of discipline are the way to life."
Proverbs 6:23

Think for a second about an exciting destination. Maybe it's the beach. Or the mountains. Or your friend's media room. Or Rome, Italy. Whichever destination comes to mind, think about how to get there from your house. If you were giving someone directions on how to find the destination, what would you tell them? What landmarks would you give them to guide them along the way?

"OK, you go past the high school, take a right at TJ's, go straight until you pass the big pond with the fountain. The stadium will be to your left."

When you are unsure of the way, or are following someone's directions, you use landmarks along the way to guide you. It's these landmarks that help get you where you need to go.

Read Proverbs 6:20–23. The author of Proverbs was preparing to warn his audience about the temptation of sexual sin. Before speaking about this issue, however, the author reminded his audience that the godly teachings passed down from parents and others served to keep them from sinful living. Verse 23 says it best: godly teachings guide us along life's journey. But godly teachings do more than that.

Think about the opening analogy of this devotional in light of verse 23. This verse speaks of "life" as the destination. The "way," or pathway, to life is literally living according to God's teachings. As you go along life's path, God's Word will be the lamp and the light you need to find your way. More than that, God's laws and rules are the way—the way to true life. Just like landmarks on the way to your favorite destination, God's Word can help guide you to where you want to go.

REFLECT

1. Do you find it easy to live a life that lines up with how the Bible says you should live?

2. What do you find hard about living this life? What do you find easy about it?

3. Have you ever turned to the Bible for help in dealing with temptation? If so, how did it help you? If not, what is keeping you from turning to it in the future?

4. Write a prayer thanking God for the guidance He has made available through His Word. Commit to turning to God's Word first when you need help through tough times.

Have you ever heard the expression, "Death is a part of living"? While it seems a bit morbid, it plays out in so many ways. Fresh flowers light up a room (and can earn you big points with that special someone in your life). But their beauty is passing; within days they wilt and decay. And who hasn't had the experience of losing that beloved pet fish, hamster, or similar "life-expectancy-impaired" animal? We can joke about losing gerbils, but what about losing people? Nothing stings like the death of someone you love. Once you experience it, life is really never the same.

Let's face it: things of this world don't last. People, plants, pets . . . they all fade. They all fail. They all die.

Read Isaiah 40:1–8. If you'll remember, Isaiah had the task of telling Israel how badly they had blown it. He hammered them by reminding them they had turned away from God. But he also gave a message of hope for the day God would restore Israel. In this passage, Isaiah relays to the people the words God has given him. In verse 6, however, another voice tells Isaiah to "cry out," or in other words, to mourn for what God has done to Israel. Isaiah basically says, "Why should I cry? Did you think you'd live forever? Don't you know that God is the only thing that lasts forever?"

While they're no fun to dwell on, loss, death, and people letting you down are a part of life. There are times in life when you will feel alone. But take heart in the words of Isaiah 40:8: God's Word is eternal. It has existed since before the beginning of time. And it will last forever. You can count on God's Word in a world where everything else will eventually fail.

God's Word will always, forever be a source of comfort and strength for you.

REFLECT

1. In what ways does God give you daily reminders of His plan and love for you?

2. Describe a time when God's Word has brought you comfort.

3. God tells us our lives on earth are temporary. How should this affect the way we live as Christians?

4. Write a prayer to God thanking Him for being a God of comfort. Express to Him your desire to better know His Word. Praise Him for providing us with an eternal source of assurance.

"Is not my word like fire," declares the LORD, "and like a hammer that breaks a rock in pieces?"
Jeremiah 23:29

Wood and rock. Wood is strong and durable. Your wooden home keeps out the wind and the rain. A wooden bridge is strong enough to hold cars. Wooden rollercoasters support an enormous amount of stress and pressure. George Washington had wooden dentures. (It's true . . . maybe.) Rock is strong and solid. Think about Dwayne "The Rock" Johnson. Pretty tough dude, right? For ages rock has been used in buildings and architecture. Medieval fortresses and castles were built with rocks. And everyone knows that rock beats scissors.

Wood and rock. Strong, durable, solid. Yet, place a match next to a bridge or rollercoaster made of wood and both would be toast. Likewise, the strongest rock is no match for a hammer and chisel in the hands of the right person.

Read Jeremiah 23:25–29. God used the prophet Jeremiah to speak judgment against Israel. In spite of all God had done for them, Israel had turned their backs to Him. In these verses, Jeremiah communicates God's displeasure over prophets who falsely claimed they spoke the truth of God. God is saying through Jeremiah that His Word had enough power to separate a true prophet from a phony.

The Word of God is not to be taken lightly. Like fire, it is a consuming force. Like a hammer, it is capable of breaking the prideful and the wicked. How? By showing the right way to live, God's Word convicts people of sin. By showing the only way to obtain salvation and life, God's Word either saves people or condemns them. By predicting the ultimate victory Christ will have over evil, and the judgment that awaits all humankind, God's Word leaves people with no excuse for not choosing to follow Him.

As a follower of Christ, God's Word can create a powerful force in your life.

1. Do you have areas in your life that don't match up with the kind of life God calls you to live? How can you look to the Bible to help you "burn away" those areas?

2. If you think of the world around you as a rock, how can you use God's Word as a hammer to break through to any friends you might have who are not followers of Christ?

3. Write a prayer to God asking Him to show you any sin in your life by revealing the truth of His Word. Thank God that He lovingly shows us the way to purpose and meaning through the Bible.

"Take the helmet of salvation and the sword of the Spirit, which is the word of God."
Ephesians 6:17

A helmet is primarily used for protection. Think about it: construction workers wear helmets, as well as bikers, skateboarders, mountain climbers, football players, race car drivers, astronauts, Army dudes, Vikings, Stormtroopers, jet pilots, and old-school deep sea divers. All of these people utilize helmets.

Swords, on the other hand, are usually used as offensive weapons. Ninjas and pirates definitely carry them. Knights have them, too. Samurais have swords, and so do cooks at those Japanese steak houses. (Not really, but that would be awesome, right?) Marines have really cool swords. So do Spartan warriors. Helmets and swords are pretty cool . . .

Read Ephesians 6:10–20. As you read this passage, don't miss the fact that Paul was teaching the great responsibility Christians have to clothe themselves in the things of the Lord. These verses show that the things of God—His truth, righteousness, salvation, and Spirit—are all necessary for navigating our daily lives. But one of the coolest things is how Paul talks about God's Word.

Paul wrote that we should pick up the "sword of the Spirit, which is the word of God" (v. 17). In your interactions with the world, the Word of God is an offensive tool you have available each and every day. If you are truly following Christ, you will encounter many discomforts in this world. As a Christian, you are called to simply "ride out" much of this trouble. (The Bible calls this "persevering.") Yet the Word of God serves as your "sword," one of the main ways you can combat the world. Is someone pressuring you to do things you know would not bring glory to Christ? Answer that person with Scripture. Feeling alone? Go to God's Word. Unsure about the world? Search for the Truth in the Bible.

You don't have to feel timid. God's Word is your best bet for answers to a sometimes-hostile world.

1. In what ways does the world try and break your spirit?

2. Take some time and pray through Ephesians 6:10–20 verse by verse. Ask the Lord for what you need today: Strength (v. 10); Truth (v. 14); Righteousness (v. 14); Peace (v. 15); Faith (v. 16); Salvation and Spirit in the Word (v. 17); Perseverance (v. 18); Boldness (v. 19).

"All Scripture is God-breathed and is useful for teaching, rebuking, correcting and training in righteousness."
2 Timothy 3:16

Think about your cell phone, assuming you have one of course. If your parents still haven't given in and bought you one, think about any cell phone in general. (This exercise is probably painful for you cell phone-less souls. But stick with it. It will be worth it in the end.) Are you thinking about it? OK, now read the following sentence describing cell phones:

> *All cell phones are battery powered and are useful for talking, texting, storing information, and performing other various functions.*

The sentence above makes two statements about cell phones: a statement about the source of their power, and a statement about their various uses. Got it? Hold on to this thought . . .

Read 2 Timothy 3:10–17. The Apostle Paul was writing to his sidekick, Timothy, a young church leader. In verses 14–17, we see Paul giving Timothy excellent advice about God's Word. In verses 14–15 Paul begins to express the importance of knowing and following Scripture. But Paul's statement in verses 16–17 is one of the most useful statements made about God's Word in the entire Bible.

The cell phone sentence you read earlier made a statement about the source of cell phones' power (their batteries), and a statement about their various uses (talking, texting, etc.). Verse 16 makes two similar statements about God's Word: a statement about the source of Scriptures' power (God), and a statement about its various uses (teaching, rebuking, correcting and training in righteousness). You can place your complete trust in the Bible's authority; after all, it is God-breathed, or, God-inspired. You can also know that Scripture is useful in your life. Don't be afraid to teach, challenge, or correct others based on Scripture. And don't be afraid to let Scripture be used for these same purposes in your own life.

1. God Himself inspired all of Scripture. God used people to record what He wanted to say. Does this change the way you look at the Bible's authority to speak into your life?

2. How might you use the Bible to correct a Christian friend? How might you use it to correct an attitude or action in your own life?

3. How are you being trained in righteousness in your life? If you do not feel satisfied with your training, do you have someone you could talk to?

4. Write a prayer to God asking Him to use His Word to teach, rebuke, and correct you. Ask the Holy Spirit to give you the strength to use God's Word in your interactions with Christian friends.

"I have not departed from the commands of his lips; I have treasured the words of his mouth more than my daily bread."
Job 23:12

There is a story about a missionary couple that adopted a poor, orphaned child from a country in Africa. When the couple picked up the sickly child from the orphanage, the child cried hysterically. On the way to the hotel the child pretty much went ballistic. The entire time she kept her right fist clenched tight in a ball. When the child's new mother attempted to unclench her fist, it only made the child cry worse. Hours later, when the child had cried herself into a deep sleep, the mother was able to pry the child's fist open. What she found inside was heartbreaking. The child had been tightly squeezing a piece of bread.

Read Job 23:1–12. If you know Job's story, you can understand his feelings here. He felt alone. He was in the middle of a huge trial. He had lost his children and his ability to make a living. He was searching for God but could not seem to find Him. But (and this is a big "but"), Job says in verse 10 that even though God seems far away, Job will remain faithful. He was confident the Lord would see him through his trials.

Verse 12 provides a glimpse into the depth of Job's desire for God. Like a starving little girl holding tightly to a piece of bread, Job was desperately clinging to God. All the girl knew was that her last piece of bread might save her life for one more day. All Job knew was that the Word of God was literally more important than food; God's Word was all that kept him going.

Just like the loving couple that swooped in and saved the little girl, God's Word came to Job and rescued him from his pain. God's Word can do the same for you. Trust in it, and God will prove Himself faithful.

REFLECT

1. Do you make being careful to follow God's commands part of your daily life? If you are like most people, you follow some commands but not others. Why is this?

2. Why is it sometimes hard for us to think about having the kind of relationship with Scripture that Job had? (Let's face it: We do not always "treasure" God's Word.)

3. How has your Bible reading been lately? What kind of attitude have you had toward Scripture? If you need to make a change, what is your plan?

4. Write or say a prayer to God confessing the fact that you may not give His Word the place of prominence it deserves in your life. Ask Him to help you obey His Word.

> "But his delight is in the law of the LORD, and on his law he meditates day and night."
> **Psalm 1:2**

What do you delight in? What really makes you happy? And don't worry about being super-Christian in your answer; be real. Is it clothes? Music? Boys? The Boston Red Sox? Maybe it is hanging out with friends. Or gaming. You might be a Hannah Montana nut, or addicted to searching for cool Facebook™ applications. Whatever it is, think for a second about why it makes you happy. What is it about your passion that makes you feel so good?

Read Psalm 1:1–3. These three verses paint a really cool picture of what it looks like to seek God and His Word. Look at verse 1. This psalm written thousands of years ago says what you know to be true today: You cannot have meaningful relationships with people who foolishly chase the ways of this world. Verse 2 continues the message. It says that the kind of people who do not hang out with the wicked are also those who find happiness in knowing God through His Word. Verse 3 finishes the picture: The person who delights in knowing and obeying the Word of God will be like a healthy, vibrant tree. God will bless this person.

Can you say that you honestly take joy in spending time with God through His Word? Don't feel guilty for the other things that bring you joy in life. God desires for you to live a full, fun life. But you may want to think about what you look to for happiness. If you look at your life and see that you put other things before your relationship with God, you need to make a change.

Finding God in His Word can truly lead to a kind of happiness you can't find anywhere else. Give it a chance. You might be surprised.

1. What are some practical, real-life examples of ways in which God's Word might bring joy to your everyday life?

2. Do you meditate on God's Word? Do you think about it day and night? If not, why not?

3. Take a few moments and pray through verses 1-3. Spend some time really dwelling on these verses. Ask God to help you recall them as you go throughout your day. Thank God for sending the Holy Spirit to help you meditate on His Word.

"I have hidden your word in my heart that I might not sin against you."
Psalm 119:11

Have you ever heard a song on the radio that kept playing in your mind all day long? Sometimes it's the last song you hear before parking your car and cutting off the engine. Or it's the song playing on the radio when your alarm goes off. This probably happens a good bit, doesn't it? You go through the day humming words or tapping your foot to the beat. You may even find yourself singing it out loud before immediately stopping once you realize people are staring. What is it about a tune that gets so deep in your mind that you can't stop thinking about it? The more you think about it . . . well, the more you think about it!

Have you ever had this scenario happen with Scripture? This isn't as far fetched as you might think. Psalm 119 actually talks a lot about this very thing: God's Word playing constantly in your mind, to the point that it becomes a part of who you are. If this concept seems foreign to you, keep reading.

Read Psalm 119:9–16. The author asks a question in verse 9: "How can a young man keep his way pure?" Verse 11 gives the answer. The challenge is for you to hide God's Word in your heart so that it is constantly on your lips and in your mind. Do you want to live a life worthy of a follower of Jesus? Then learn and follow His Word. God's words are pure, insightful, and true. Knowing and obeying them is what we are called to do as followers of Christ. These verses remind us that God's ways are pure and that they help us not sin against Him.

Think today about how seriously you take the call to seek, understand, and remember God's Word.

1. Write down three verses from memory. How does your ability or inability to do this reflect how well you've hidden God's Word in your heart?

2. Why is it important to know and remember God's Word?

3. What things in your life stand in the way of you being more dedicated to memorizing God's Word?

4. Here is a challenge: Write down today's verse two times in the space provided below. Try to remember it as you go throughout your day. When you go to bed tonight, see if you can remember it. (Here's the trick . . . If you do this little exercise, you are practicing what it means to "meditate" on God's Word. If you make this practice a habit, you will find yourself longing to know more Scripture.)

> "Open my eyes that
> I may see wonderful
> things in your law."
> **Psalm 119:18**

Do you know someone who has just started following Christ? One of the coolest things about interacting with someone young in their faith is seeing their hunger for God's Word. So many new Christ-followers are hungry to know more of God through reading the Bible. But some new believers struggle because they don't really know how to study God's Word. The Bible is pretty big. Some wonder, "Where am I supposed to start?"

Read Psalm 119:17–24. In this passage, the author proclaims his devotion to God. The tone of this passage is worth paying attention to. Doesn't the author almost seem uncertain to you? We get a hint from verse 23 that maybe things aren't going so well. In a time of some sort of hardship, it's as if the author is saying to God, "I am trying to obey you as best I know how in the midst of a big mess. Please show me how I can obey you more." It's the picture of someone who really desires to follow after God.

The safe bet is that you want to follow God, too. (After all, you wouldn't be reading this book if you didn't.) But even though you want to follow Him, do you ever get confused about what God expects from you? If so, then Psalm 119:18 is a great verse to meditate on. The Bible is full of so much truth, so many places where God reveals amazing teachings to us. Sometimes it's hard for us to figure out exactly what we are supposed to do with all the great stories and teachings in the Bible. Psalm 119:18 is a great verse to pray when you feel confused about God's Word.

When you ask the Lord to show you His ways, He will open your eyes to many things you've never seen before in His Word.

1. Why do you, a 21st century teenager, sometimes have trouble understanding God's Word? What do you do when you don't understand something?

2. Have you ever prayed and asked the Lord to help you know what the Word is saying to you (v. 18)?

3. Has God's Word ever been a source of wonder for you? Describe a time, or an experience in which God's Word came alive in a wonderful way.

4. Journal a prayer in the space below asking the Lord to open your eyes to what He wants you to know and learn.

"When your words came, I ate them; they were my joy and my heart's delight, for I bear your name, O LORD God Almighty."
Jeremiah 15:16

Think for a moment what it means to "bear" someone or something's name. When you wear your high school's name on a t-shirt or jacket, you bear your school's name. An athlete who plays for a sports team bears the name of that specific organization or school. When you give your name to someone, you are representing your parents, and your parents' parents, and your parents' parents' parents . . . OK, you get the picture. And regardless of whether or not you want the responsibility, the way you act is a reflection of your family; you can either bring them honor, or shame.

Here's a challenge. If you really want to get the full picture of Jeremiah 15:16, Read Jeremiah 15:1–16. Did you read it? Seems harsh, right? God had given Jeremiah a message of judgment and punishment. God used Jeremiah to warn the Israelites of the consequences for their disobedience. By the time you get to Jeremiah's words in verse 15, we get the picture of why Jeremiah was a pretty unpopular guy. In verse 15, Jeremiah says, "I have had a rough time, God, because of the words you told me to speak."

But the cool thing about verse 16 is that even though he knew God's words would make him unpopular, Jeremiah eagerly accepted them. Why? Because he bore the name of God. Because he had a relationship with God, Jeremiah delighted in God's Word, even though it wasn't always pleasant.

Sometimes God's Word can be a bitter pill to swallow. We are sinful people. Our hearts will always lean toward sin. God's Word calls us to righteousness. Sometimes that will make us uncomfortable. But because we are God's children, we bear the name of Christ. Because we bear the name of Christ, His Word should bring us joy. And we should desire to honor Him with our lives.

REFLECT

1. How do you know you "bear" Christ's name? How do you know you are one of God's children?

2. How can you "delight" in God's Word even though it sometimes seems tough to follow?

3. How would you describe the hunger you have for God's Word? Are you satisfied with your desire to know God?

4. Write a prayer asking God to increase your desire for His Word. Pray that the Holy Spirit will give you power to live in a way that brings honor to God.

Jesus answered, "It is written: 'Man does not live on bread alone, but on every word that comes from the mouth of God.'"
Matthew 4:4

Taylor is a pretty smart guy, and he is super responsible. He's got everything going for him. One of the things he has going for him is a really cool car. Taylor's car is red . . . and fast. It has really nice rims and really expensive tires. Taylor knows how cool his car is. He washes it. He vacuums it. He makes sure it always has enough gas, wiper fluid, and power-steering fluid in it. But Taylor never remembered to put oil in it. And one day as Taylor was driving his cool, fast, red car down the road, his engine caught fire and blew up. You see, Taylor's car can't run on gas alone.

Read Matthew 4:1–4. Jesus was under much temptation from Satan. But Jesus could have just turned Satan away, right? Let's be clear: Jesus is powerful enough to have sent Satan running. But keep in mind that while Jesus was fully God, He was also fully human. To completely relate to us, His creation, Jesus allowed Himself to be tempted. He had just fasted 40 days and Satan was tempting Him with food, questioning both His power and His will power. But Jesus trusted in the Father's Word to provide and sustain Him.

While it's important that Jesus experienced and resisted temptation, it's equally important for us to look at His example and see *how* He resisted. Jesus placed major value on God's Word. He understood that people could have everything, but if they did not have God and His Word, their lives would ultimately be meaningless. Just like Taylor's cool sports car wouldn't run without oil, you cannot have a fruitful life without God and His Word.

Jesus turned to God's Word to help Him resist temptation. You can turn to God's Word for help in getting you through any situation in life.

1. Why is it potentially dangerous for people to think they can get through this life all on their own, with no help from God or anyone else?

2. Give some examples of how you depend on the Lord daily?

3. What sort of temptation have you endured lately? Have you let God sustain you in that temptation or have you given in to the temptation?

4. Journal a short prayer asking the Lord to give you faith to live on every word that comes from the mouth of God.

"But these are written that you may believe that Jesus is the Christ, the Son of God, and that by believing you may have life in his name."
John 20:31

Tests are lame. They are the speed bumps on the joyride of high school. Think about it: if not for tests, school wouldn't be that bad. Even if you hate tests, you have to admit that you understand their purpose. The purpose of tests is to see if you have really learned what you need to learn. Why is that important? Because high school has a purpose, too: to prepare you for life after high school. Whether you plan on going to college, to the military, to work a trade, or to Africa to work for a non-profit, the purpose of high school is to give you the knowledge and experience to be able to succeed at the next level. While at times it can seem like the purpose is to drain the life out of you one lunchroom meal at a time, the purpose is actually much more beneficial.

Read John 20:24–31. John the Apostle was one of the disciples. He wrote the Book of John, along with the Book of Revelation, and 1, 2, and 3 John. In John 20, he records several of the appearances Jesus made after rising from the dead. And in verse 31, John gives the reason he recorded these appearances: John wanted his readers to know what Jesus did so that they might believe He was the Son of God. John understood that this belief in Jesus leads to eternal life.

Just like high school has a purpose, God's Word has a purpose. The purpose of the Bible is to reveal God's plan to redeem humankind from sin. As followers of Christ, we know that this redemption comes through Jesus. God gave the Bible to us so we would know Him and believe in Him as a result.

While high school might prepare you for life, God's Word is life. Follow His Word and live.

1. Why do we sometimes resist the very things that are meant to help us? (For example: school, studying God's Word)

2. How do the stories in the Bible help keep your faith strong? Describe some times in your life when you have had to rely on the things you learned from the Bible.

3. If God's Word is the means of leading you to faith in Christ, can you afford to take your commitment to it lightly? What are the consequences of not knowing God's Word?

4. Write a prayer to God thanking Him for the life He gives through His Son, Jesus. Commit today to be more aware of the life He has given you. Ask God to show you how you can live for Him today.

"I am not ashamed of the gospel, because it is the power of God for the salvation of everyone who believes: first for the Jew, then for the Gentile."
Romans 1:16

Here's a little game for you: name all of the dynamic duos that come to mind. On your mark, get set, go! (See how many you can come up with in 30 seconds.) Done? Good. How many did you come up with? 10? 20? Does your list include Batman and Robin? Troy and Gabriella? Curious George and the Man with the Yellow Hat? Shrek and Princess Fiona? Zack and Cody? Spaghetti and Meatballs? Barbie and Ken? If so, you're pretty good.

While there are some things you could never imagine apart (when you hear peanut butter what do you think of? Right . . . jelly), there are some things you can never imagine together. (Did you think Gorgonzola cheese when you heard peanut butter? Didn't think so.) In today's passage, Paul deals with two things that had traditionally been kept far apart.

Read Romans 1:4–17. Paul was a Jew. He grew up in the Jewish faith. And Jews were not allowed to have anything to do with Gentiles (non-Jews). When Paul was radically transformed after his encounter with Christ, he received a special mission: to take the life-changing message of Jesus to the Gentiles. Paul was determined to remind his audience that both the Jews and the Gentiles were sinful people who needed a Savior.

Nothing could keep Paul from talking about Jesus. His whole life was aimed at helping others see what an amazing life they could have in Jesus Christ. As a follower of Christ, this should be your attitude! God has given you so much. He commands that we act faithfully and obediently in return. The challenge for you is to bravely serve as a representative of Jesus and the difference He has made in your life.

REFLECT

1. What barriers keep you from speaking out about your relationship with Jesus?

2. If you are honest with yourself, do you consider some people in your school to be off-limits? What can you do to change your attitude?

3. Describe a time you've been hesitant to stand up for Jesus because you were afraid of what people would think or say.

4. Write a short prayer asking God to give you boldness like Paul. Include any specific challenges you're facing for which you need extra courage and God's strength.

> "For you have been born again, not of perishable seed, but of imperishable, through the living and enduring word of God."
> **1 Peter 1:23**

Have you ever heard of the Fountain of Youth? Many cultures have a legend focusing on a mysterious fountain with magical healing powers. These curious legends date back to the Middle Ages, and span across cultures throughout Europe, Asia, and the Caribbean. While the stories differ slightly, each tells of a fountain with unique water that can grant eternal youth to those who drink from it. The Spanish explorer Juan Ponce de León was said to have died while searching for the Fountain in the New World. Recently, magician David Copperfield claimed to have found a life-giving fountain in a group of islands he purchased in the Bahamas. Copperfield claims near-dead bugs that come into contact with the water become fully-alive and fly away. (Yeah . . . sure.)

Read 1 Peter 1:13–23. Peter was one of Jesus' most trusted disciples and one of the leaders of the New Testament Church. 1 Peter is a letter written to followers of Christ living throughout the regions of the Roman world. In this passage, Peter focuses on how Christians are to live in holiness. In verse 23, Peter sums up the reason followers of Christ are able to live a holy life: believers have been born again into new life in Christ.

As a follower of Christ, you are living in the midst of the most amazing source of eternal life. If you believe Jesus is who He said He was, and give your life to Him, you are given the gift of living forever with God. Your life will be hidden in Jesus for all of eternity. And unlike a famous explorer, you don't have to search the remote corners of the world. The way to life is right in front of you in God's Word.

REFLECT

1. What is it about human nature that makes people search for ridiculous things such as the Fountain of Youth?

2. How does knowing that you will have an eternal life in Christ after you die affect the way you live today?

3. How is your new life in Christ different from your old life, before you were "born again"? If you can't really see any difference, what does that say about the way you live your life as a Christ-follower?

4. Say or write a prayer to God expressing your great thanks for His perfect gift of eternal life with Him. Ask the Holy Spirit to help open your eyes as you study truth found in the Bible.

"Consequently, faith comes from hearing the message, and the message is heard through the word of Christ."
Romans 10:17

Have you ever been asked to work on a group project? Maybe it was a science project or a group presentation at school. If given the choice to choose your group, don't you usually pick people you can trust, people you have faith in to help you complete the project? How do you know certain people will be hard workers? It's usually because you've seen their faithfulness and have seen them prove themselves. It's hard to have faith in people who you haven't seen being faithful before.

It can work the same way when dealing with Christianity. Faith is often described as belief in things you cannot see. When we talk about faith in Christ, this definition of belief in the unseen applies. But Christ left us a book of truth and proof. The Bible gives us reason to believe and encouragement to act upon what God has asked of us. Why? Because we know He is faithful and always standing ready to give us the power to complete the tasks He gives us.

Read Romans 10:12–17. The Greek word for *word* in verse 17 literally means "a speech, or a command" and denotes the "all-powerful word or command of God." There are a lot of connections in this passage about the Word of God being spread to others, and the way it's spread is through people taking the Word and telling others. This is God's commission to us: We are to go spread His Word! The benefit of us telling others about God's story and His Truth is that it brings others to faith! God wants His people to hear the message.

1. Think of two of your friends who are not Christians. How can you share God's message with them? How can you help them understand the importance of faith in Christ?

2. Why is it important to tell others what the Word says?

3. Why is faith a result of hearing God's Word?

4. Pray and ask God to give you open eyes to see His people that need to hear His Word. Pray to the Spirit to give you the strength to be a bold witness, and the words through which to show people the light of Christ.

"For what I received I passed on to you as of first importance: that Christ died for our sins according to the Scriptures."
1 Corinthians 15:3

Think about the last incredible piece of information you received. What was it? Maybe you made first chair in the band. Or maybe you made a big play in a scrimmage. Maybe you got accepted into the college of your dreams. Or maybe it wasn't good news at all. Maybe you got detention for talking in class. Or maybe your grandmother's cancer returned. Regardless of the actual specifics of the news, there is something about human nature that makes us want to share. And not just with anyone. We usually seek out someone we are really tight with, a friend or coach, maybe even a youth minister or parent. We're just not wired to keep news to ourselves, whether good or bad.

Paul was just like us. When he had great news, he needed to share it with someone. Read 1 Corinthians 15:1–11. Paul loved the Corinthians dearly, but he was frustrated with them. You see, the believers in the Corinthian church had abandoned a lot of the teachings Paul had taken the time to impart to them. He was writing them to try and shake them up a bit, but also to give them instructions on how to live as followers of Christ.

The secret to what Paul wanted to communicate to his friends in Corinth can be seen in verses 1–2. Paul knew his message was important. What was his message? Simply that Jesus is Lord; believe in Him and be saved. Like a friend with a great bit of news, Paul could not keep his message a secret. He knew that the message of Christ saves lives. He could not contain his excitement.

Do you share Paul's excitement for telling others the amazing story of Jesus? If you believe there is no real life apart from Jesus, shouldn't you be excited to share that news?

1. What activities/sins in your life do not match up with the gospel and Scripture?

2. Why are Christ's death, burial, and resurrection of "first importance"? (vv. 3–4)

3. Why was it important for Paul to point out that all these things were written in the Scriptures?

4. Evaluate your lifestyle and commitment to Christ by asking God to take away habits and sins that do not belong in a Christian's life. Take a few minutes to pray right now and journal some thoughts in the space below.

"And you also were included in Christ when you heard the word of truth, the gospel of your salvation. Having believed, you were marked in him with a seal, the promised Holy Spirit."
Ephesians 1:13

Have you ever paid money to get into an amusement park or a county fair and had your hand stamped? The stamp on your hand is proof that you satisfied the requirements of entry. It says to anyone who might want to know that you have been accounted for. You're in.

Read Ephesians 1:13. Paul is writing to what could arguably be called his favorite group of believers, the church in Ephesus. There is so much implied in this verse; Paul describes a really cool, really dynamic process. Let's unpack it . . .

First, Paul said that his audience "heard the word of truth." Paul then explained what this word of truth was. He said the word of truth was the "gospel of [their] salvation." We know that Paul was talking about the life-changing story of Jesus. He doesn't stop there. We find a clue about the response of the church. Paul said they heard and they believed! The word of truth took hold in their heart. And what was the result of their belief? They were "marked with a seal, the promised Holy Spirit." Paul is referring to the Holy Spirit who dwells in every believer at the moment they profess faith in Christ. What an amazing amount of truth packed into one small verse.

The word of God is salvation; it is a means by which we are eventually saved from our sins. How? Because God's Word teaches us about the person of Jesus and the work He did on this earth. We hear the Word and believe in Jesus. Amazing. But there is also a great promise in this verse—the Holy Spirit comes to every believer and acts as God's seal on us. It's as if God looks at us and says, "This ones mine. This one belongs to me."

REFLECT

1. If you believe in Jesus and have submitted your life to his lordship, Scripture tells us the Spirit of God now lives inside of you. Write down a few words that describe how this makes you feel.

2. What does it mean to you to be "included in Christ"? How is your life different now that you are a part of God's family?

3. God has marked you as His. Describe how you represent Him to the world through your words and actions.

4. Pray that the Holy Spirit, who dwells in you, would give you the power today to live in a way that brings God honor. Ask the Spirit to help you make the right decisions and to make the most of the opportunities you have been given.

"How can a young man keep his way pure? By living according to your word."
Psalm 119:9

Have you ever changed a tire? With services like OnStar® and AAA™ there's a good chance you haven't. But if you have, you know there is a right way to do it. First, you loosen the lug nuts with the tire iron. Then, you jack up the car until the tire is completely off the ground and finish removing the lug nuts. Then, you remove the tire and put the spare on. Once you put the spare on, you simply tighten the lug nuts and release the jack. Once the jack has been removed, give the lug nuts one more go with the tire iron, and, viola . . . one tire change completed.

There is a right way to change a tire. There is also a wrong way. If you jack up the car and then try to loosen the lug nuts, you may knock the car off the jack. If you don't tighten the lug nuts one last time after you have finished putting on the spare, you run the risk of having your tire come off while you're driving. Not good.

Read Psalm 119:9-12. Here is a picture if a young man yearning for God. Look at those powerful emotionally charged phrases: "I seek you with all my heart." "Do not let me stray from your commands." "I have hidden your word in my heart." The author clearly desires to live as God would have him live.

Just as there is a right way to change a tire, there is a right way to live as God wants you to. How? The key is in verse 9: "by living according to [God's] word." You cannot live a good, or pure, life through your own means. Only by living according to God's words in Scripture, through the power of the Holy Spirit, can you walk in purity and holiness.

Is Scripture your guide?

REFLECT

1. How do people try to find goodness and meaning apart from a life devoted to Christ? Is this the right way or the wrong way?

2. Define in your own words what it means to be pure as a 21st century teenager.

3. What verses will you use to help you live "according to God's Word"? Write one or two down, even if you have to search through your Bible to find them.

4. Write or say a prayer asking the Holy Spirit to keep the idea of purity front and center in your mind. Ask for the Spirit's power to avoid temptations that lead you to acting impurely.

"Therefore everyone who hears these words of mine and puts them into practice is like a wise man who built his house on the rock."
Matthew 7:24

Do you have a little brother, sister, niece, or nephew who likes to play with wooden or LEGO® blocks? If so, you have probably watched them build a tower or another tall structure. The taller the tower, the more it begins to wobble. If the child is lucky, the tower hangs around long enough to get destroyed by a well-placed flying roundhouse kick. If the child is not lucky, the tower gets so wobbly that it crashes to the floor. If you watch young children build these structures, you'll quickly notice one thing: in most cases, these tall towers have a very shaky foundation. As the kids build higher, the tower simply does not have a base sturdy enough to support its weight.

Read Matthew 7:24-27. Matthew records Jesus teaching about the necessity of having a great foundation. The metaphor of solid rock vs. shifting sand speaks to the idea of faith and obedience. Verse 24 tells us that hearing the Word of the Lord and obeying what it says is a characteristic of a wise man. Those who do not take the Word seriously are called foolish.

This passage is about obedience; it's about doing, not just listening, to God's Word. But it's not just about obedience. It's also about being prepared. We must be prepared for the trials and storms that come into our lives. We as Christians are not promised a smooth life without trouble. We live in a sinful world with consequences. Knowing God's Word and living through obedience to His commands prepares us for trials.

How much time do you spend in the Word? Do you practice obedience to God's Word?

1. Compare your faith to Jesus' metaphor. Is your faith "rock solid" or "soft as sand"?

2. How can trials make your faith stronger?

3. Describe how you grew closer to Christ through a tough time in your life.

4. Write a prayer to God asking Him to show you where your foundation needs repair. Ask the Spirit to show you any weak areas you need to shore up. Thank God for His Word.

> "But the one who received the seed that fell on good soil is the man who hears the word and understands it. He produces a crop, yielding a hundred, sixty or thirty times what was sown."
> **Matthew 13:23**

Consider a seed. Any seed will do. For the sake of clarity, let's consider an apple seed. Everyone has seen an apple seed. They are small. You could hold hundreds in the palm of your hand. Yet, there is great possibility in this little seed. It has the capability to reproduce itself over and over again. Plant this seed in the ground and over time, given the right conditions, a tree will emerge. On that tree will be other apples, full of other seeds capable of producing other trees full of other apples . . . You get the point, right? A small, seemingly insignificant seed has tremendous power.

Read Matthew 13:1–23. (Yeah, it's long . . . but you'll love it.) Jesus is teaching in a parable, or a story. In this parable, Jesus set up an analogy. In His analogy, Jesus compared the Word of God to a seed. Where the soil was not suitable for a seed to grow, the seed was either eaten or it sprouted but later died. Where the soil was fertile and healthy, the seed grew and thrived . . . and would go on to produce more fruit that would produce more seeds . . . and on, and on, and on.

Is your heart fertile? Is your heart healthy soil? Is your heart a place where the seed of God's Word can put down roots and grow strong? You know, you don't have to answer this question. It can be answered by looking at your life. Does your life produce fruit? Do you draw people to God? Do you serve others in Jesus' name?

Make it your priority to have a heart full of good soil.

1. Describe what you think it means to have a heart of good soil.

2. If your heart is rocky, what do you need to do to make it a better environment for God's Word to grow?

3. Where do you see fruit in your life? What is the evidence of God's Word being active in you?

4. Make a list of three of your friends who are not followers of Christ. Pray that they would hear God's Word and that it would find their hearts to be fertile soil.

He replied, "Blessed rather are those who hear the word of God and obey it."
Luke 11:28

There are different sorts of crowds, aren't there? Think about the last large crowd you were around. Was it a football game? A concert? Maybe you were at the mall. Or maybe you have a very large church. Regardless, each crowd behaves differently. The crowd at a Hannah Montana concert would be very different from the crowd at a high school graduation. Crowds can be fun, quiet, loud, scary . . . you name it. The one thing that is consistent about a crowd is that you can't miss it. By nature, they are quite noticeable.

Jesus always drew a crowd, and you can bet that crowd was loud! Jesus' teachings intrigued people and they wanted to be near Him. Some people mocked Him, some people praised Him, and others were merely watching in wonder trying to figure out what He was offering.

In Luke 11:27-28, we read of Jesus hearing a woman above all the other noise in the crowd. Jesus responded to this woman (who was praising Jesus' mother) by letting her know that it is not anyone's place to be blessed and praised for that reason. Jesus goes on to say that we are blessed when we hear the Word of God and obey it!

The word blessed is used in this context to describe someone who is not blessed because they have any external, worldly privilege, but because they have the Spirit of God alive and living in their heart. This is not a state of material happiness, but a state of being fulfilled in Christ. Jesus makes it clear that obedience is the key to being blessed. God's Word is a crucial part of knowing obedience to Christ. The challenge is to "hear the Word of God and obey it."

1. What's one thing in God's Word you have trouble obeying? Why do we have trouble obeying God's Word?

2. Do you feel "blessed" as this devotional defines it?

3. How can you become more satisfied in Christ?

4. Journal a short prayer asking God to bless you and fill you with His satisfying love.

To the Jews who had believed him, Jesus said, "If you hold to my teaching, you are really my disciples."
John 8:31

Can you imagine what it must have been like to be one of the first people to fly into space? We're not as impressed with space travel as we once were, but imagine the excitement and uncertainty the first astronauts felt. What about the first guys to take a submarine for an underwater adventure? Or the first person to parachute out of a plane? Can you imagine the thrill? It's one thing to believe in the possibility of these things. But what amazing confidence these people must have to actually try the space ship, or the submarine, or the parachute . . .

Read John 8:31-39. Jesus could count on opposition from the Jews. The Jews were God's chosen people. They lived according to the laws and teachings of God given to them thousands of years before Jesus came on the scene. Many Jews simply would not allow themselves to believe Jesus was the Messiah, the promised Son of God. But there were many Jews who did believe. In verse 31, Jesus taught them what it really looked like to be one of His followers.

The first guy to ever jump out of a plane with a parachute on his back exhibited an extreme amount of faith in that thin, round piece of silk. He completely put his trust in the one thing capable of saving his life. If he said he believed in the use of parachutes, but never was willing to put his life on the line by jumping out of a plane, then it would be easy to dismiss his belief. The same is true with our faith in God. If we say we believe, yet do not obey the teachings of Christ given to us in the Bible, then we have to ask if we really do believe Jesus is who He says He is.

Are you a follower of Christ?

REFLECT

1. Describe the last really tough time you went through. What did you hold to? Family? Friends? God? Something else?

2. How were you able to get through the tough time?

3. What did you learn about your faith? Why is it that trials or difficult circumstances can sometimes make our faith grow deeper?

4. Ask God to help give you a passion for His Word. (After all, you cannot hold to Christ's teachings if you don't know what they are.) Commit to memorizing John 8:31.

"Let the word of Christ dwell in you richly as you teach and admonish one another with all wisdom, and as you sing psalms, hymns and spiritual songs with gratitude in your hearts to God."
Colossians 3:16

Think about the idea of *dwelling*. Webster's™ gives this definition: "to remain for a time," or "to live as a resident." You can dwell on a hard decision. You can dwell on a great memory—that Homecoming dance last year with "you know who," or the time you scored the winning goal. You can dwell on a relationship gone right . . . or gone wrong. You can dwell in a house. You can dwell in the mall. (Some of your parents would probably like it if you dwelled a little *less* at the mall.) What you will learn today is that you have the opportunity to allow God's word to dwell in you.

Colossians 3:1-17 gives a great picture of how a Christ-follower should act, think, and live. Take a look at the passage and keep in mind the joy God gives us through this new life of salvation! It's not about rules and regulations; it's about "setting your mind on the things above, not on the things that are on earth" (Col 3:2). When your thoughts and actions are filtered through the teachings of Scripture, love, unity, and peace are the result (vs. 14-15). Verse 16 shows us what the overflow of Christ's joy produces—gratitude. We teach, admonish (literally meaning to "put into the mind"), sing Scripture back to Christ who gives us such joy through His Word and life.

Take time today to meditate on God's Word and dwell on the thought of God's wisdom. God's Word is living and active. It will dwell in you if you will only take the time to read it and think on it. Remember that gratitude is a result of having his Truth dwell in your heart.

Thank God for His Word today!

1. What are some instructions from Colossians 3:1-17 that are hard for you to practice?

2. How does your life show gratitude to God?

3. List some people who exemplify a life of praise to God. How can you learn from these people you listed? What are some qualities of these people you'd like to have in order to give God praise?

4. Read Colossians 3:1-17 one more time and meditate on the encouragement and instruction Paul gives. As you read, pray that God will help you put these things into practice.

"Do your best to present yourself to God as one approved, a workman who does not need to be ashamed and who correctly handles the word of truth."
2 Timothy 2:15

Kim was going to the beach for a few days with her mom. It was going to be an awesome time for the two of them to just chill out together—no school, no work, no practice . . . just a relaxing weekend by the pool. Kim wanted to be sure she had her poolside entertainment lined up. The problem was her iPod™ was broken. Before she left, she asked her friend Erica if she could borrow hers. Erica was cool with it, so Kim headed to the beach, iPod in tow. All was well until that afternoon when Kim's mom suggested they go take a dip in the ocean. As Kim got up, Erica's iPod tumbled out of Kim's lap and into the pool. Kim stared in disbelief as her best friend's mp3 player sunk slowly to a watery death on the bottom of the shallow end.

Now, did Kim mean to destroy Erica's iPod? Of course, not. But that doesn't change the fact that it was absolutely trashed. And when Kim had to sheepishly call her friend and inform her of the tragedy, it didn't matter if it was intentional or not. As far as Erica was concerned, Kim had made a huge mistake. She was careless with her stuff. Even though Kim promised to replace the iPod, Erica couldn't help but feel kind of sad, and a little angry. Kim couldn't help but feel ashamed.

Read 2 Timothy 2:15. Paul is helping his right-hand-man, Timothy, to understand one thing: there is a right way to handle God's Word. It is to be treated with the utmost respect. It is to be given a place of authority in our lives. It is to be respected. And it is to be loved.

How are you handling the Word?

1. In your own words, list some ways you can handle God's Word correctly.

2. Now, think of some ways an individual might handle God's Word incorrectly.

3. The word ashamed is pretty strong. Why would anyone be ashamed of being a follower of Christ?

4. Take a moment to pray for two things—that God would help you live today as one He could approve of, and that you would be bold for Christ, choosing not to be ashamed.

"Preach the Word; be prepared in season and out of season; correct, rebuke and encourage—with great patience and careful instruction."
2 Timothy 4:2

Professional athletes get paid millions of dollars to perform their skills at the highest level. For months at a time, throughout their seasons, these athletes push their bodies to the limits week after week, sometimes night after night. When the season is over, nearly every one of these athletes take some well-deserved downtime to let their bodies heal. They rest. They relax. Then, most resume their training months ahead of the next season so they will be prepared to perform once again. However, some athletes take too much time off. Each year there are reports of athletes showing up to their pre-season camps overweight and out of shape. They have failed to prepare for the season.

Read 2 Timothy 4:1-5. As you have already learned, Paul's letters to Timothy contain a lot of practical instruction. They were written from an older, wiser man to a young, vibrant church leader. In this passage, Paul is warning Timothy to be watchful of people who water down God's Word. Paul said that people would change God's Word to say what they wanted to hear. We face the same issue today. In order to fight this, just as Paul warned, we must be *prepared* by knowing God's Word.

A professional athlete has a season, a defined time where he or she is expected to perform. As a follower of Christ, you don't have a season. Every day is game day! You have to be prepared in season and out. Prepared for what? Prepared to be a person who brings the truth of God's Word into a lost world.

You can't do it if you don't know it. And you can't know it unless you study it. Don't let today go by without studying God's Word.

1. What opportunities do you encounter each day where you can somehow mention Scripture?

2. How can you be prepared for these opportunities?

3. How can you use Scripture to encourage a friend who is down?

4. Have you ever had the opportunity to correct someone's actions or attitudes based on Scripture? If so, were you prepared?

"Do not merely listen to the word, and so deceive yourselves. Do what it says."
James 1:22

Imagine a teenage guy cruising along down the Interstate—windows down, music up. He sees something that causes him to slow down. It's a police officer stopped in the road waving her arms with the car lights on. The guy stops and rolls down his window. "Just wanted you to know the bridge is out up ahead," the officer kindly says. "Whew! Thank you for telling me, officer," he replies, proceeding to slam his foot down on the gas and peel off, barreling straight towards the collapsed bridge.

This story makes no sense, right? Why? Because if the guy were really given such instruction, he would pay attention; he would listen to the warnings and then obey them. In this type of scenario, everyone would heed the potentially lifesaving advice.

Why is it sometimes different with God's Word?

Read James 1:21-24. What is the first thing you see? Verse 21 says it takes humility to accept the Word of God. You see, humans struggle with thinking we know it all. But it is not enough to merely listen to the word and know what it says, is it?

Quite clearly verse 22 says that if you are only hearing God's Word and not putting it into action, you are fooling yourself. Like the guy speeding towards a broken bridge, full speed ahead, ignoring God's teachings will only lead to disaster. You must hear God's Word and then let it impact every part of your life. These verses call you to live a life that reflects the teachings of the Bible.

REFLECT

1. Are there parts of your life you have yet to truly surrender to God? If so, write these areas down in the space provided.

2. What is keeping you from humbling yourself before God and allowing Him to take over every area of your life?

3. List three changes you need to make in your life to begin to know God's Word as well as you know your own reflection.

4. Write a prayer in the space below asking God to help you commit to better knowing and applying His Word in your life.

"I write to you, fathers, because you have known him who is from the beginning. I write to you, young men, because you are strong, and the word of God lives in you, and you have overcome the evil one."
1 John 2:14

Chances are, you know God. And it is very likely that you are a follower of Christ. If you weren't, you probably wouldn't be reading this book.

You know that God is the Father, the almighty creator of the universe. He is the Alpha and the Omega, the first and the last. He hung the stars in the heavens. He set the mountains on their foundations. The sea hits the shores because He set its boundary.

You know that Jesus is God's only Son, chosen before time to be the One through whom all of God's children would be redeemed. He was born in the most humble surroundings and raised in a small corner of the world. Yet, He is the Christ, the Lamb of God, Messiah, Savior.

Think for a moment how you know God. Think how you know Christ. While God chooses to reveal Himself through His creation, and through His Spirit, the primary way God speaks to us is through His Word. You know Him because you read about Him in the Bible.

In 1 John 2:14, John recognizes that his readers knew God, that they were strong in their faith, and that they had overcome the devil. The only way this was possible for John's audience was because the Word of God lived among them.

You have the Word of God living in you, too. Be encouraged. Take heart. You are a child of God, and His truth dwells in you. You have overcome the world through Jesus! Never be timid or scared . . . be bold! The Spirit of God is with you always.

1. Who first taught you about God? About His Son, Jesus? Do you recall any of the stories this individual taught you? What was it about those stories that captured your attention?

2. How has your faith and knowledge grown as you have grown?

3. How do you react to the fact that you have overcome the devil's hold in your life? How did you overcome this?

4. Write a prayer to God today thanking Him for the gift of His word. Thank Him for communicating to you. Thank God for assuring that your future is with Him.

CLOSING

And here you are . . .

You have reached the end. Good for you; it's a good sign that you stuck with it to the finish. It means you can keep a commitment. That's what it takes to *know* God's Word. Commitment. And that's what it takes to *live* according to God's Word.

Commitment.

This is your goal as you grow in your faith and in your understanding of God and His ways. Stay committed to the task at hand. There is a saying, "Nothing worth having comes easy." This simple saying is a great summary of your life as a Christ-follower. It will not be easy. But every moment of it is worth it. So, as you get ready to put this book down for the last time (or at least the last time for a while . . .), leave with this challenge ringing in your ears:

Commit yourself to reading and learning God's Word. It is truly the bread of life. It will serve as a guide every day of your life.

Commit yourself to praying the words of Scripture. Choose passages of the Bible and pray them as if they were your words. Praise God with the same praises written by David, Hannah, or Mary.

Commit yourself to living out the truth you read in God's Word. It is silly to read the Bible then turn and live your life as if you had never touched its pages. Let the Word of God transform you. Live according to its teaching.

Finally, commit to having Scripture on your lips. What does that mean? As you go throughout this life, let God's Word season your interactions with others. Look for instances where you can speak Bible verses into a conversation. By doing this, you will show the world that God's Word has relevance in your life. You would be surprised at the impact this can have on people.

Thank you for spending time with this book. But don't stop here. Keep growing in your knowledge and understanding of God's Word.

ABOUT the AUTHORS

Andy Blanks
Andy is originally from Auburn, AL, but lives in Birmingham. He is married and has three daughters. Andy will receive his Master's of Divinity from New Orleans Baptist Seminary in 2009. In his 31 years on this earth, Andy has worked as a farm hand, served in Iraq with the Marines, done missionary work in China, and grown gourmet mushrooms in a top-secret factory (Seriously). Andy loves writing, speaking to youth and college groups, and cheering on his beloved Boston Red Sox to ever increasing on-field glory.

Melanie Dill
Melanie grew up in Snellville, GA and now resides in Birmingham, AL. She graduated from Samford University in 2004 with a Graphic Design degree. In her spare time, she likes to paint, read, workout, and play with her dog, Pickles. Melanie collects turtle art and coffee cups. But not coffee art. Or turtle cups.

Executive Editor
Andy Blanks

Copy Editor
Kaci Hindman
Ann Claire Vaughn

Art Director
Mike Robinson

Graphic Designer
Zack Nichols

Publishing Assistant
Brooke Culpepper
Staci Caldwell